Name Faith

P9-CAR-964

Flip Fun!
Choose five capital letters. Write five names that begin with each letter.

1

0-88012-826-7 • Traditional Cursive

Name _____

a   *d*   *g*

a a a a
a a a a
a a a a a a a a a a a
d d d d d d d d d d
d d d d d d d d d d
g g g g g g g g g
g g g g g g g g g g
aaaa dddd gggg

q q q q q

q q q q q

q q q q q q q q q q

o o o o o o o o o

o o o o o o o o o o o o o o

c c c c c c c c c

c c c c c c c c c c

qqqq   oooo   ccccc

3

© Carson-Dellosa   4   0-88012-826-7 • Traditional Cursive

i i i i i

i i i i

i

u u u u u u u u u u

u

e e e e e e e e e

e

i i i i i   u u u u u u u u   e e e e

W AV av

AV AV AV

av

S AV AV AV AV AV AV AV

AV

r AV AV AV AV AV AV AV

AV

AV AV AV AV AV AV AV AV

6 Brooklyn

n n n n n n n

n n n n n n

n u u u u u u

m m m m m m m m

m g g g g g

y y ny ny ny ny ny ny

ny y y y y y

m m m m m m m ny ny ny

7

0-88012-826-7 • Traditional Cursive

Name _____

Name _____

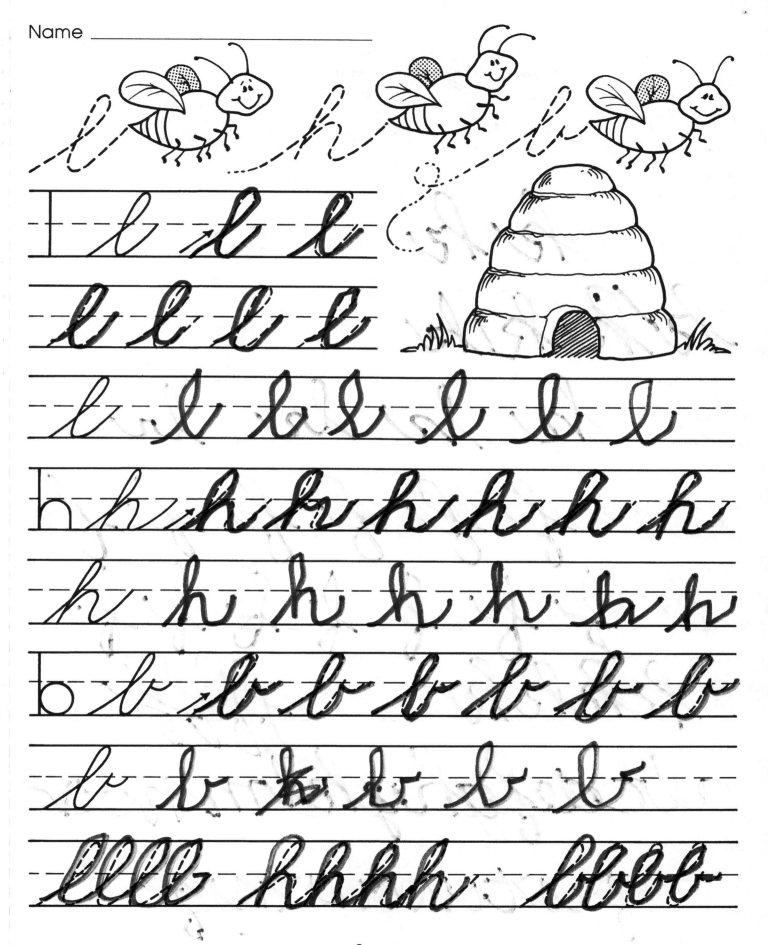

9

0-88012-826-7 • Traditional Cursive

k k k k k

k k k k k k

k k k k k k

f f f f f f f f f f

f f f f f f f f f f

k k k k k   f f f f

a b c d e f g h i j k l m n o p

q r s t u v w x y z

Name _____

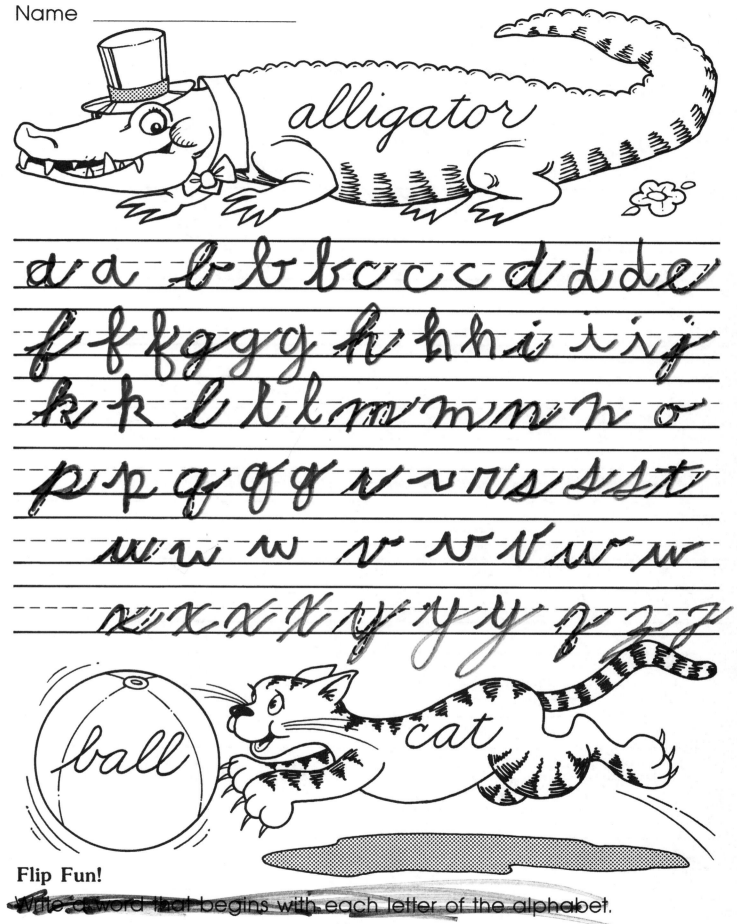

alligator

a a b b c c d d d e

f f g g g h h h i i i j

k k l l l m m n n o

p p q q q r r rs s s t

u u u w w v v v u u w

x x x x y y y y z z z

ball

cat

Flip Fun!

Write a word that begins with each letter of the alphabet.

11

0-88012-826-7 • Traditional Cursive

Name _____

0-88012-826-7 • Traditional Cursive

Name _____

P B G S

P P P P P P P

P

B B B B B B B

B

G G G G G G G

G

S S S S S S S

S

13

0-88012-826-7 • Traditional Cursive

Name _____

© Carson-Dellosa

0-88012-826-7 • Traditional Cursive

Name _____

Name _____

16
0-88012-826-7 • Traditional Cursive

Name _____

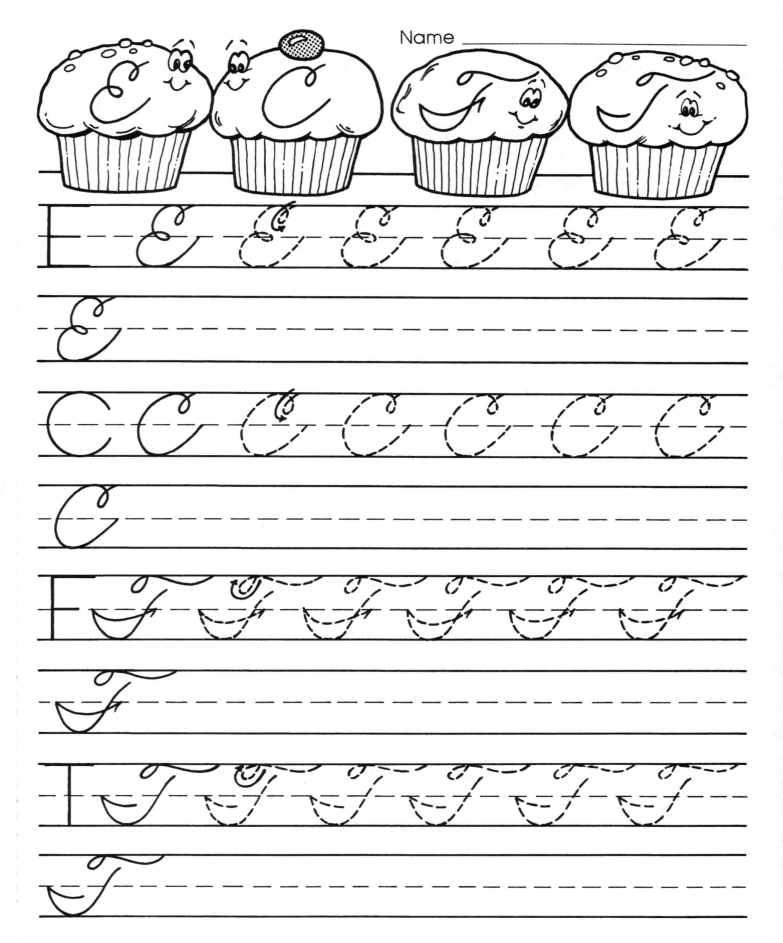

0-88012-826-7 • Traditional Cursive

Name _____

Name

A B C D E
F G H I J
K L M N O
P Q R S T
U V W
X Y Z

0-88012-826-7 • Traditional Cursive

Name _____

Aa Bb Cc

Dd Ee Ff

Gg Hh Ii

Jj Kk Ll

Mm Nn Oo

Pp Qq Rr

Ss Tt Uu

Vv Ww Xx

Yy Zz

Flip Fun!
Write a sentence using as many different letters as possible.

20   0-88012-826-7 • Traditional Cursive

Name _____

𝒜 𝒜 𝒜 𝒜 𝒜

α α α α α

𝒜α 𝒜α 𝒜α

𝒜 𝒜

α α

𝒜 α 𝒜α

alfalfa   Arizona   afraid

Amanda   appear   animal

Appalachia

algebra

almanac

Here's my best!   𝒜   α

Flip Fun!

Write the nine **A** words from above in alphabetical order.

CLAP!   CLAP!

A A A A A A A A A

a a a a a a a a a a

A a A a

Antarctica

astronaut

Amazing aerial acrobats

always accept applause.

Flip Fun!
Look up the meaning of aerial. Use the word in a sentence.

B B B B B B B

b b b b b b

Bb Bb Bb Bb

B B

b b

Bb Bb

bubble Barbara baboon

Boston baseball baby

Bermuda

barbeque

blackberry

Here's my best! B b

Flip Fun!

Use each capital **B** word in a sentence.

Name _____

B B

b b

B b B b

Barbados

billboard

Busy, bronze bees buzz

beautiful buttercups.

Flip Fun!
Write another sentence about bees using at least four **B** words.

0-88012-826-7 • Traditional Cursive

Name _____

C C C C C C C

C C C C C C

Cc Cc Cc

C C

c c

Cc Cc

cocoon   Chicago   circle

Candice   cat   character

Colorado

chicken

church

Here's my best! C   c

Flip Fun!
Write five people names and one country name that begins with **C**.

Cc

Cc

Cc Cc

California

coconut

Clever circus clowns

create crazy cartoons.

Flip Fun!
Write three statements about California.

Name _____

Dd Dd Dd Dd Dd

d d d d d d

Dd Dd Dd

DD

d d

Dd Dd

doodle David demand

deserted dawdle Daddy

Detroit

dedicate

dream

Here's my best! D   d

Flip Fun!

Doodle a picture about a boy named David.

27

Dd

dd

Dd Dd

Delaware

dachshund

Dieting dinosaurs don't

devour delicious desserts.

Flip Fun!
Look up the meaning of deceptive. Use the word in a sentence.

$\mathcal{E}$ $\mathcal{E}$ $\mathcal{E}$ $\mathcal{E}$ $\mathcal{E}$ $\mathcal{E}$

ℓ ℓ ℓ ℓ ℓ ℓ ℓ

$\mathcal{E}e$ $\mathcal{E}e$ $\mathcal{E}e$

$\mathcal{E}\mathcal{E}$

ℓ ℓ

$\mathcal{E}e$ $\mathcal{E}e$

electric   Earth   everyone

Elizabeth   eagle   energy

Eskimo

elephant

event

Here's my best! $\mathcal{E}$ _____ ℓ

Flip Fun!

Write three sentences which contain a traced word from above.

0-88012-826-7 • Traditional Cursive

E E

e e

Ee Ee

Europe

evergreen

Educated elephants

exercise energetically.

Flip Fun!
Write three new sentences about educated elephants.

Name _____

F F F F F F F

f f f f f f f

F f F f F f

F

f f

F f F f

fifty France fruitful

Fifty forefathers fife

Finland

forceful

frankfurter

Here's my best! F f

Flip Fun!
Look up the meaning of forefather. Use the word in a sentence.

Name _____

$\mathcal{F}$

$f\ f$

$\mathcal{F}\ f\ \mathcal{F}\ f$

$\mathcal{F}lorida$

$firefly$

$\mathcal{F}antastic\ fudge\ fills$

$four\ fat,\ friendly\ frogs.$

Flip Fun!
Use the letters in the **F** words above to write six new **F** words.

© Carson-Dellosa

32

0-88012-826-7 • Traditional Cursive

Name _____

G G G G G G G

g g g g g g g

Gg Gg Gg Gg

G G G G G G G G G G

g g g g g g g g g g g g g g

Gg Gg

gadget   Greece   gateleg

George   gauge   garbage

Georgia

gingerbread

garage

Here's my best!   G   g

Flip Fun!

Write three questions about Greece.

33

    0-88012-826-7 • Traditional Cursive

G G

g g

G g G g

Gettysburg

gingham

Grouchy gorilla grabs

giggling girl's gum.

Flip Fun!
Use each word above in a separate sentence.

H H H H H H H

h h h h h h h

Hh Hh Hh

H H

h h

Hh Hh

headache Harvard hat

hazard high Harvey

Holland

hitchhike

heart

Here's my best! *H h*

Flip Fun!

Write the **H** words in alphabetical order.

Name _____

HOLLYWOOD

$\mathcal{H}\ \mathcal{H}$

$h\ h$

$\mathcal{H}h\ \mathcal{H}h$

Honolulu

highchair

Hip Hollywood hogs

hum harmoniously.

Flip Fun!
Write a paragraph about Hollywood.

Name _____

i i i i i i

i i i i i i i i

I i I i I i

I i

i i

I i I i

inflict iris initiative

brain island Inca

Italian

intelligible

incision

Here's my best! I i

Flip Fun!

Look up the meaning of initiative. Use the word in a sentence.

37

0-88012-826-7 • Traditional Cursive

Il

ii ii

Ii Ii

Illinois

identification

Indestructible insects

invade irate Indians.

Iip Fun!

Write another sentence about indestructible insects.

$\mathcal{J}$ $\mathcal{J}$ $\mathcal{J}$ $\mathcal{J}$ $\mathcal{J}$ $\mathcal{J}$

j j j j j

$\mathcal{J}j$ $\mathcal{J}j$ $\mathcal{J}j$

$\mathcal{J}$ $\mathcal{J}$

jj

$\mathcal{J}j$ $\mathcal{J}j$

justice Jupiter jogging

Jo-Jo jester juvenile

Japan

jalopy

juke box

Here's my best! $\mathcal{J}$ j

Flip Fun!
Write three statements about Jupiter.

0-88012-826-7 • Traditional Cursive

Name _____

JJJ

jjj

Jj Jj

Jamaica

journal

Jubilant, jumping

jaguars juggle junk.

Flip Fun!
Use each J word in a separate sentence.

40 0-88012-826-7 • Traditional Cursive

K K K K K K K

k k k k k

Kk Kk Kk

K K

k k

Kk Kk

kaleidoscope Kay kenifer

kettle Korea knowledge

Kansas

kangaroo

ketchup

Here's my best! K k

Flip Fun!
Draw the design you would like to see in a kaleidoscope.

Kk Kk

kk kk

Kk Kite Kk

Kentucky

knuckle

Kindergarten kids keep

kooky knickknacks.

Flip Fun!
Write a sentence about what you might find in a kid's knapsack.

$\mathcal{L}$ $\mathcal{L}$ $\mathcal{L}$ $\mathcal{L}$ $\mathcal{L}$ $\mathcal{L}$

l l l l l

$\mathcal{L}$ l $\mathcal{L}$ l $\mathcal{L}$ l

$\mathcal{L}$ $\mathcal{L}$

l l

$\mathcal{L}$ l $\mathcal{L}$ l

logical Lillian llama

Lima laughable lagoon

Louisiana

landlord

lyrical

Here's my best! $\mathcal{L}$ l

Flip Fun!
Use the letters in the L words to write six new L words.

L L

l l

L l L l

Louisville

little

Large, lazy lizards

lick lemon lollipops.

Flip Fun!
Write another sentence about large, lazy lizards.

m m m m m m m

m m m m m m m

Mm Mm Mm

M M

m m

Mm Mm

member Mimi medium

Memphis monkey mime

Manhattan

madam

marmalade

Here's my best! M   m

Flip Fun!
Write the names of two states which begin with **M**.

M M

m m

Mm Mm

Mayflower

memorize

Mischievous mosquitos

make mice mad.

Flip Fun!
Write one sentence about mighty mammoths and one sentence about
mischievous mice.

n n n n n n n n

m m m m m m m

Nn Nn Nn

Nn

m

Nn Nn

nation Nebraska mine

Nancy nonsense none

Nevada

neon

nineteen

Here's my best! *N*   *n*

Flip Fun!

Write nine new **N** words.

Nn

nn

Nn Nn

Netherlands

nanny

Neptune's nephew needs

nourishment nightly.

Flip Fun!
Look up the meaning of navigates. Use the word in a sentence.

Name _____

𝒪 𝒪 𝒪 𝒪 𝒪 𝒪 𝒪

𝓸 𝓸 𝓸 𝓸 𝓸 𝓸

𝒪𝓸 𝒪𝓸 𝒪𝓸 𝒪𝓸

𝒪𝓸

𝓸 𝓸

𝒪𝓸 𝒪𝓸

opportunity Ohio aloe

Ollie opossum o'clock

Oklahoma

onion

opposite

Here's my best! 𝒪 𝓸

Flip Fun!
Write five sets of words which are opposites.

© Carson-Dellosa

49

0-88012-826-7 • Traditional Cursive

Name _____

$\mathcal{O\!O}$ — — — — — — — — —

$\sigma\ \sigma$

$\mathcal{O}\sigma\ \mathcal{O}\sigma$ — — — — —

$\mathcal{O}ntario$ — — — — — —

$octagon$ — — — — — —

$\mathcal{O}rating\ owls\ offer\ odd$

$opinions\ on\ opera.$

Flip Fun!
Write three odd opinions an old owl might give.

Pp Pp Pp Pp

pp pp pp pp

Pp Pp Pp

Pp

pp

Pp Pp

people Phoenix purple

Penelope pop puppy

Philadelphia

pineapple

pumpkin

Here's my best! P p

Flip Fun!

Use each P word in a sentence.

Name _____

P p

p p

P p P p

Philippines

pepper

Polite, pink pigs pour

peach punch properly.

Flip Fun!
Write a sentence about pink pigs and purple pickups.

0-88012-826-7 • Traditional Cursive

Q Q Q Q Q

q q q q q

Q q Q q Q q

Q Q

q q

Q q Q q

quilt quarter quiver

Quincy quick quack

Quixote

quicksand

quarterback

Here's my best! Q   q

Flip Fun!
Write three statements about quicksand.

Q Q

q q

Q q Q q

Quebec

question

Quiet quail quartet

quells queen's qualms.

Flip Fun!
Look up quells and qualms. Use each word in a sentence.

Name _____

RRRRRRR

rrrrrrrr

Rr Rr Rr

RR

rr

Rr Rr

railroad Robert river

Rachel reindeer record

Rhodes

refrigerator

reward

Here's my best! R   r

Flip Fun!
Write the **R** words in alphabetical order.

R R

r r

Rr Rr

Rome

raspberry

Rusty robots require

repeated repairs.

Flip Fun!

Write a paragraph about robots.

0-88012-826-7 • Traditional Cursive

Name _____

Ssssss Ss

Ss Ss Ss Ss Ss

Ss Ss Ss

Ss

ss

Ss Ss

Susan sassy sarcastic

seamstress Steve sand

Scotland

seesaw

spider

Here's my best! *S* *s*

Flip Fun!
Write six new **S** words. Use each word in a sentence.

Ss

Ss

Ss Ss

Switzerland

season

See slippery, snoring

snails sleep soundly.

Flip Fun!
Use each word in the sentence above in a separate sentence.

Name _____

𝒯 𝒯 𝒯 𝒯 𝒯

𝓉 𝓉 𝓉 𝓉 𝓉

𝒯𝓉 𝒯𝓉 𝒯𝓉

𝒯𝒯

𝓉 𝓉

𝒯𝓉 𝒯𝓉

twenty Tara tickets

talent tiptoe Thomas

Texas

tapestry

totem

Here's my best! 𝒯 ___ 𝓉

Flip Fun!
Write three questions about totem poles.

F F

t t

Ft Ft

Tibet

trumpet

The top turtle took

two tennis trophies.

Flip Fun!
Write five things you want to do when you become a teenager.

0-88012-826-7 • Traditional Cursive

Uu Uu Uu Uu Uu

uu uu uu uu uu

Uuu Uuu Uuu

Uu

uu

Uu Uu

uniform Uranus up

usually union umpire

United States

utopia

urgent

Here's my best! U   u

Flip Fun!
Write the **U** words in alphabetical order.

0-88012-826-7 • Traditional Cursive

U U

W W

Uw Uw

Utah

unusual

Unforgettable unicorns

unfurl umbrellas.

Flip Fun!

Write three statements about unicorns.

0-88012-826-7 • Traditional Cursive

Name _____

𝒱 𝒱 𝒱 𝒱 𝒱 𝒱 𝒱

𝓋 𝓋 𝓋 𝓋 𝓋 𝓋 𝓋

𝒱𝓋 𝒱𝓋 𝒱𝓋

𝒱𝒱

𝓋 𝓋

𝒱𝓋 𝒱𝓋

vitamin Vivian vase

Victor vivacious video

Vermont

verve

vivid

Here's my best! 𝒱 𝓋

Flip Fun!

Choose three **V** words above. Use each in a sentence.

63 0-88012-826-7 • Traditional Cursive

$\mathcal{V}\ \mathcal{V}$

$v\ v$

$\mathcal{V}v\ \mathcal{V}v$

$\mathcal{V}ancouver$

$velvet$

$\mathcal{V}acationing\ visitors$

$view\ volatile\ volcano.$

Flip Fun!
Write a paragraph about volcanoes.

0-88012-826-7 • Traditional Cursive

W W W W W

w w w w w w w

War War War

W W

w w

War War

world Wilma whisper

William wheel worm

Wyoming

worthwhile

well-wisher

Here's my best! W w

Flip Fun!
Write the **W** words in alphabetical order.

0-88012-826-7 • Traditional Cursive

W W

w w

Wa Wa

Washington

watchword

White whales wonder

where walruses winter.

Flip Fun!
Write a sentence about a whale and a sentence about a walrus.

X X X X X X X

XXXXXXXXXXXXX

Xx Xx Xx

X X

x x

Xx Xx

x-ray Xerxes xiphoid

xylophone Xavier Xmas

Xerox

x-axis

xenophobe

Here's my best! X   x

Flip Fun!
Use three X words in a sentence.

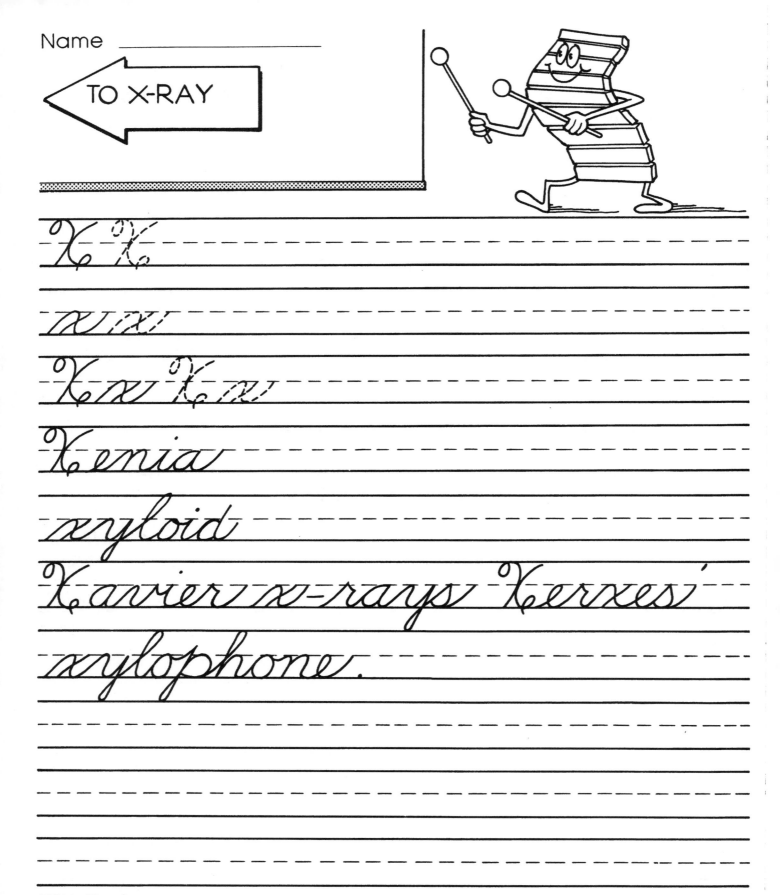

Name _____

TO X-RAY

𝒳 𝒳

𝓍 𝓍 𝓍

𝒳 𝓍 𝒳 𝓍

Xenia

xyloid

Xavier x-rays Xerxes'

xylophone.

Flip Fun!

Write another sentence about a xylophone.

0-88012-826-7 • Traditional Cursive

Y Y Y Y Y Y Y Y

y y y y y y y y

Yy Yy Yy

Y Y

yy

Yy Yy

yogurt Yolanda yarn

yearbook young Yukon

Yorktown

yellow

youth

Here's my best! Y   y

Flip Fun!

Write a paragraph about *you* for your school yearbook.

Yy Yy

yy yy

Yy Yy

Yellowstone

yo-yo

Young, Yankee yeoman

yells, "Yonder!"

Flip Fun!

Look up the meaning of yeoman. Use the word in a sentence.

Z Z Z Z Z Z Z

Z Z Z Z Z Z Z

Z Z Z Z Z

Z Z

ZZ ZZ

zoom   zodiac   zinnia

zucchini   Zeus   Zack

Zambia

zero

zest

Here's my best! Z   z

Flip Fun!

Write the **Z** words in alphabetical order.

𝓩 𝓩

𝓩 𝓩

𝓩 𝓩 𝓩 𝓩

Zurich

zipper

Zimbabwe's zany zebras

zigzag zealously.

Flip Fun!
Write two more sentences about other things zebras might do in the zoo.

0-88012-826-7 • Traditional Cursive

Numerals and Number Words

1 2 3 4 5 6 7 8 9 0

Trace and write.

1 one

2 two

3 three

4 four

5 five

6 six

7 seven

8 eight

9 nine

10 ten

Flip Fun!

Write a sentence using each odd number.

Name _____

Days of the Week

Friday   Wednesday

Sunday   Thursday

Tuesday   Monday

Saturday

Write the days in order two times.

_____

_____

_____

_____

_____

_____

_____

_____

_____

Flip Fun!

Choose your favorite day of the week. Write a paragraph about how you like to spend that day.

Trace and write.

Months of the Year

January

February

March

April

May

June

July

August

September

October

November

December

Flip Fun!
Write a sentence about one winter month and one summer month.

Name _____

About Me

Write your . . .

Name.

_____
- -

Street number and name.

_____
- -

City, state and zip code.

_____
- -

Area code and telephone number.

_____
- -

School.

_____
- -

Three favorite school subjects.

_____
- -

Three favorite sports.

_____
- -

Three favorite foods.

_____
- -

Favorite TV program.

_____
- -

Favorite book.

_____
- -

Flip Fun!
Write a paragraph about a typical school day.

Name _____

Draw your family.

Trace and copy.

father

mother

brother

sister

Write a sentence about your family.

Name _____

This sentence has every letter from A-Z.

Trace.

The quicker brown fox jumps over the lazy dog.

Copy.

Copy.

Write A-Z.

Write A-Z.

Flip Fun!
Write ten words that have six or more letters.

0-88012-826-7 • Traditional Cursive

SENTENCES

Name _____

The school play is today.
Copy.

Did you buy a ticket?
Copy.

Meet me at seven o'clock.
Copy.

The curtain is rising!
Copy.

© Carson-Dellosa790-88012-826-7 • Traditional Cursive

CHALLENGE

Write a word with...

one syllable

two syllables

three syllables

four syllables

three letters

four letters

five letters

six letters

two e's

two o's

ing

er

The Liberty Bell

The Liberty Bell is a true symbol of American independence. The famous bell was rung in 1776 to celebrate the signing of the Declaration of Independence. Cracked in 1835, today the bell hangs in the Liberty Bell Pavilion in Philadelphia.

Copy.

_____

_____

_____

_____

_____

_____

_____

_____

The Pledge of Allegiance

The Pledge of Allegiance is a solemn oath of loyalty to the United States. The original pledge was first recited by school children in 1892.

In 1954, the words "under God" were added to the pledge, the salute to the American flag.

Copy.

The Washington Monument

The Washington Monument
was built in honor of George
Washington. It stands by the
Potomac River in Washington,
D.C. Covered with white marble,
it rises 556 feet in the air.
Visitors to the monument must
ride an elevator to get to the top.

Copy.

Capitol Hill

Capitol Hill is perhaps the best
known area in Washington, D.C.
Several important government
buildings are on Capitol Hill,
which rises 88 feet in the center
of the city. (Some buildings are:
U.S. Capitol, Library of Congress
and Supreme Court Building.)

Copy.

The Pony Express

The Pony Express was an amazing mail delivery service that carried mail across the 1,966 miles between Missouri and California.

Established in 1860, the Pony Express consisted of 400 fast horses, 80 riders and 190 stations.

Copy.

Camp David

Camp David is the official retreat for the President of the United States. It is built on the heavily-wooded Catoctin Mountain in Maryland.

Camp David has been a home away from the White House since 1942.

Copy.

The Constitution

The Constitution is the set of laws which governs our country. The Constitution was signed on September 17, 1787, at Independence Hall in Philadelphia.

It explains the aims of our government and lists the rights of each American citizen.

Copy.

Old Ironsides

The Constitution, better known as "Old Ironsides", is the oldest warship afloat in the world.

Old Ironsides was launched in 1791 and fought in the War of 1812. Now docked at the Navy Yard in Boston, the ship underwent reconstruction in the 1800's.

Copy.

The Library of Congress

The Library of Congress, located
in Washington, D.C., is one of the
largest libraries in the world.
It contains over 77 million items,
including 18 million books and
pamphlets.

Established in 1800, it includes
3 buildings with 71 acres of space.

Copy.

The American Eagle

The American Eagle is the
official national bird of the
United States. It was selected
by Congress in 1782.

The American Eagle is found
in all parts of North America.
It has white head, neck and tail
feathers, and brown body feathers.

Copy.

The Declaration
of Independence

The Declaration of Independence, signed on July 4, 1776, was a formal announcement that declared our country free from Great Britain's rule. Written by Thomas Jefferson, it stated that the 13 colonies were becoming a new nation, the United States of America.

Copy.

The Jefferson Memorial

The Jefferson Memorial is dedicated to the memory of America's third President.

The memorial was dedicated on April 13, 1943, on the 200th anniversary of Jefferson's birth.

The white marble building holds a 19-foot statue of Jefferson.

Copy.

The Smithsonian
Institution
The Smithsonian Institution
is a collection of museums, art
galleries, laboratories, a zoo and
educational programs for the
people. Founded in 1846, the
museums display everything
from diamonds to reconstructed
dinosaurs.

Copy.

The California Gold Rush

The California Gold Rush began on January 24, 1848, when gold was discovered at Sutter's Mill. As the news spread, people rushed to California by the thousands to look for gold. This westward movement aided in developing the frontier.

Copy.

Niagara Falls

Niagara Falls is one of the most spectacular natural wonders in North America. A popular tourist attraction, the falls connect Lake Ontario and Lake Erie. Over 12 million cubic feet of water a minute pour over the falls.

Copy.

The Lincoln Memorial

The Lincoln Memorial stands in Washington, D.C. in honor of Abraham Lincoln, our country's sixteenth President. Dedicated in 1922, the Memorial is 80 feet tall, 189 feet long and 118⅔ feet wide.

The center of the monument holds a gigantic statue of Lincoln. Engraved on the walls surrounding the monument are the Gettysburg Address, Lincoln's most famous speech, and his Second Inaugural Address.

Copy.

The United States Capitol

The United States Capitol is the building where Congress conducts our government's business. It stands on Capitol Hill in Washington, D.C. The 540-room building is famous for its domed roof. The dome covers the Rotunda, a huge round room in the Capitol's center. To the south of the Rotunda is the House of Representatives. The Senate is on the north side of the Rotunda.

The Capitol was built in the 1790's. Each year, over 10 million people visit this important building.

Copy.

The Gettysburg Address

Name _____

    The Gettysburg Address was a famous speech given by President Abraham Lincoln on November 19, 1863. He spoke at Gettysburg, Pennsylvania, the site of a famous Civil War battle. In his speech, Lincoln honored those who had bravely fought and died in the Battle of Gettysburg.

    Although the speech was very brief, it is one of the most famous in history. The entire speech is carved on a stone plaque on the wall of the Lincoln Memorial in Washington, DC.

Copy.

"The Midnight Ride of Paul Revere"

Name _____

During the Revolutionary War, Paul Revere was a famous silversmith in Boston. On April 18, 1775, British troops were ordered to attack Concord, a nearby town.

Paul Revere arranged for a special signal to be flashed from the steeple of the Old North Church. Two lanterns meant the Redcoats were coming by sea, and one lantern meant they were coming by land. At one a.m., Paul Revere rode by horse to Concord warning people that the British troops were coming. A famous poem has been written about his ride.

Copy.

Mount Vernon

Mount Vernon was the home of George and Martha Washington. The mansion stands on a high bluff overlooking the Potomac River in Virginia.

Washington lived at Mount Vernon before he was called to lead the Continental Army in the Revolutionary War in 1775. After his Presidency, Washington returned to live at Mount Vernon. Both George and Martha Washington are buried on the Mount Vernon estate.

Copy.

The Brooklyn Bridge

Name _____

The Brooklyn Bridge, built in 1883, spans the East River in New York City. The 1,595-foot long bridge connects Brooklyn and Manhattan.

It took 14 years to build, and was at that time the largest suspension bridge in the world.

The bridge hangs from steel cables which are fastened to two 275-foot towers located at each end of the bridge. The bridge cost 15 million dollars to build in the late 1800's.

Copy.

© Carson-Dellosa   0-88012-826-7 • Traditional Cursive

The Erie Canal

The Erie Canal, completed in 1825, was the most important national waterway built in the United States. The canal was valuable because it joined the Great Lakes with the Atlantic Ocean.

Built across the state of New York, the canal allowed goods to be shipped east and west. But gradually, as railroads were built across the country, the canal became a less important means of transporting goods.

Copy.

The Mount Rushmore National Memorial

The Mount Rushmore National Memorial is a huge carving on a granite cliff in the Black Hills of South Dakota. The famous carving shows the faces of four American Presidents: George Washington, Thomas Jefferson, Theodore Roosevelt and Abraham Lincoln.

Work began on the Mount Rushmore National Memorial in 1927 and was completed 14 years later in 1941. The first President to be completed was Washington whose carved head is 60 feet tall!

Copy.

The White House

The White House is the official residence of the President of the United States. This 132-room mansion contains family rooms as well as the Oval Office, where the President carries out the country's business each day.

Many of the rooms at the White House are open for public tours. The Red Room and the State Dining Room are among the public's favorites. The address of the White House is 1600 Pennsylvania Avenue.

Copy.

_____

_____

_____

_____

_____

_____

_____

_____

_____

The Battle of Bunker Hill

The Battle of Bunker Hill is one of the most famous battles of the American Revolution.

On June 16, 1775, colonial troops took Breed's Hill, close to Bunker Hill. The next morning, the British marched up the hill twice, but the colonists held the hill. The third time, the colonists ran out of gunpowder and lost the hill. In spite of their loss, the colonists were proud that they had fought so hard against the British troops.

Copy.

The Star-Spangled Banner

Name _____

"The Star-Spangled Banner" is the national anthem of the United States. It was written by Francis Scott Key during the War of 1812.

On Tuesday, September 13, 1814, the British navy attacked Fort McHenry. Key, who was being held prisoner on a British ship, watched the attack all through the night. At dawn, Key saw the American flag still waving over Fort McHenry. He was so thrilled that he wrote the words that we now sing as our national anthem.

Copy.

Monticello

Monticello was the private home of America's third President, Thomas Jefferson. Located on a hilltop near Charlottesville, Virginia, the mansion was designed by Jefferson himself.

Jefferson planned Monticello in 1768. By 1770, construction had begun. In 1775, Jefferson moved into his new home.

Jefferson loved to invent new ways to use things. Many of his inventions are found in Monticello, including a swivel chair, enclosed bed and revolving buffet.

Copy.

The Transcontinental Railroad

The Transcontinental Railroad was the first coast-to-coast railroad in the world. Until 1869, America did not have a railroad west of the Mississippi. Congress asked that one railroad be built from the east and one from the west. Soon the two railroads were in a race to see which could lay the most track in the shortest time.

On May 10, 1869, the tracks came together in Promontory, Utah, to form the first coast-to-coast railroad.

Copy.

The American Flag

The American flag was adopted on
June 14, 1777. The first flag contained 13 red
and white stripes and 13 white stars on a
field of blue. The 13 stripes and stars stood for
the 13 American colonies. No one knows who
made the first flag, although many believe
that it may have been Betsy Ross.

In 1818, it was decided that a new star
would be added for each new state. Known
as the Stars and Stripes, the American flag
now has 50 white stars, one for each of the 50 states. It has not
changed since July 4, 1960, when Hawaii became a state.

Copy.

_____

_____

_____

_____

_____

_____

_____

_____

_____

_____

_____

_____

The President
of the United States

The President of the United States is the head of the executive branch of government. Often called the chief executive, the President has many important duties. Among them, the President must make sure all federal laws are enforced and must oversee national defense.

To become President, a person must have been born in the United States and be at least 35 years old. The President's term of office is four years, and he/she may only serve two consecutive terms.

If a President dies in office, or for some reason cannot perform the duties, the Vice President becomes President.

Copy.

_____

_____

_____

_____

_____

_____

_____

_____

_____

_____

_____

_____

The Congress of the United States

The Congress of the United States is the legislative branch of the federal government. Its most important job is making laws.

Congress is made up of two groups: the Senate and the House of Representatives. Two senators are elected from each state giving the Senate 100 members. Senators are elected every six years. The House of Representatives has 435 members. Representatives are elected every two years.

The two groups meet in the Capitol building in the Senate or House chambers. They serve as direct representatives of the American people.

Copy.

_____

_____

_____

_____

_____

_____

_____

_____

_____

_____

_____

_____

The Supreme Court
of the United States

The Supreme Court of the United States heads the judicial branch of the federal government. As the highest court in the land, it is responsible for upholding the laws of the country.

The Supreme Court is the only court created by the United States Constitution. It is made up of nine members — a chief justice and eight associate justices. The justices, appointed by the President, must be approved by the Senate. They serve for life or until retirement.

The Supreme Court spends much of its time determining the meaning of the laws of the Constitution. It settles many court cases based on these laws.

Copy.

_____

_____

_____

_____

_____

_____

_____

_____

_____

_____

The Boston Tea Party

Name _____

The Boston Tea Party is one of the most famous events in America's history. In 1767, the British government placed a high tax on tea and other items sent to America. This harsh tax meant that some colonists would go out of business. Many patriotic colonists decided to protest the unfair tax.

On the night of December 16, 1773, a group of loyal colonists, dressed as Indians, boarded three British ships in Boston Harbor. They dumped 342 chests of tea into the water. This action inspired many colonists to work together for a free country.

Copy.

_____

_____

_____

_____

_____

_____

_____

_____

_____

_____

_____

_____

_____

The Statue of Liberty

Name _____

The Statue of Liberty stands on Liberty Island at the entrance to New York Harbor. The colossal statue is of a woman, dressed in a robe, holding a torch high above her head in her right hand. In her left hand, she holds a book of law inscribed July 4, 1776.

The over 150-foot high copper statue was a gift of friendship from the people of France to America in 1884. The statue has become a symbol of freedom to people around the world.

In the early 1980's, repair work was begun on the statue. By 1986, the Statue of Liberty celebrated its 100th birthday by standing completely restored.

Copy.

_____

_____

_____

_____

_____

_____

_____

_____

_____

_____

_____

_____

Carlsbad Cavern

Carlsbad Cavern is an amazing system of caves and tunnels located near Carlsbad, New Mexico. The cavern contains thousands of beautiful stalactites hanging from the ceiling, and stalagmites rising from the floor.

The cavern extends over 1,000 feet below ground in some places and covers almost 47,000 acres. The largest area in the cavern is called the Big Room, measuring 1,800 feet long.

Visitors to the cavern are allowed to tour a three-mile route underground. On summer nights, they can watch millions of bats fly from the Bat Cave to hunt insects. After eating about eleven tons of insects throughout the night, they return before dawn to sleep.

Copy.

_____

_____

_____

_____

_____

_____

_____

_____

_____

_____

_____

The Grand Canyon

The Grand Canyon, which stretches for 277 miles, is one of the great natural wonders of the world. Located in northwest Arizona, it is home for over 120 kinds of animals, such as mountain lions, elk, bighorn sheep and antelope. The Colorado River flows through the center of the canyon.

The Grand Canyon National Park was formed in 1919. The park covers 1,218,375 acres! Over two-and-one-half million people visit the canyon each year. Visitors are allowed to take a mule ride through the canyon, or ride by boat or raft on the Colorado River. Some visitors may even choose to hike into the canyon — a 21-mile trip!

Copy.

_____

_____

_____

_____

_____

_____

_____

_____

_____

_____

_____

_____

_____

_____

Sequoia National Park

Name _____

The Sequoia National Park is located in the Sierra Nevada Mountains of California. The largest tree in the world, the General Sherman Tree, can be found in this park. This giant sequoia stands 275 feet high and measures 103 feet around its base. It is believed that this tree could produce over 600,000 board feet of lumber.

young tree   maturing tree   old tree

The giant sequoia is an evergreen tree. Scientists are able to determine the age of these trees by counting their growth rings. The General Sherman Tree is believed to be between 2,200 and 2,500 years old, which makes it one of the oldest living things on Earth.

Copy.

_____

_____

_____

_____

_____

_____

_____

_____

_____

_____

_____

_____

_____

The Original Thirteen Colonies

Name _____

The original thirteen colonies were founded in America between 1607 and 1733. The thirteen colonies, located on the Atlantic Coast, were: Virginia, Massachusetts, New Hampshire, New York, Connecticut, Maryland, Rhode Island, Delaware, Pennsylvania, North Carolina, New Jersey, South Carolina and Georgia.

Most of the early colonists came to this country to seek a better life. Many colonists hoped for better jobs. Many wanted to own their own land. Others came to the colonies to enjoy freedom of worship.

Copy.

_____

_____

_____

_____

_____

_____

_____

_____

_____

_____

_____

_____

_____

The Alamo

The Alamo was the site of a famous battle fought in 1836. Located in San Antonio, Texas, the Alamo was built as a church mission in about 1718.

During the winter of 1835-1836, the people of Texas fought Mexico for their independence. General Santa Anna of Mexico brought his troops to San Antonio. The Texans found safety behind the walls of the Alamo. On February 23, 1836, the Mexican army attacked the Alamo.

Some believe that all the Texans who fought died in the battle. Others believe Davy Crockett, the legendary frontiersman from Tennessee, survived the battle only to be executed at Santa Anna's orders.

Copy.

_____

_____

_____

_____

_____

_____

_____

_____

_____

_____

_____

_____

The First Moon Landing

Name _____

On July 20, 1969, America's spacecraft, Apollo II, landed on the moon. Astronaut Neil A. Armstrong was the first person to step on the moon's surface.

Until this time, only unmanned spacecraft had journeyed to the moon. Photographs from these flights helped scientists plan the exact spot where Apollo II should land.

There were several later Apollo missions to the moon. Apollo 15 astronauts even rode on the moon in a special car called a lunar rover!

All lunar astronauts gathered samples and information for future study of the moon.

Copy.

The Tomb of the Unknowns

Name _____

The Tomb of the Unknowns, in Arlington, Virginia, honors all who have given their lives in service to America during war.

On Armistice Day, November 11, 1921, the body of an unknown soldier was buried in the Arlington National Cemetery. The soldier was killed in World War I. Since that date, unknown soldiers from the Vietnam War, the Korean War and World War II have been buried beside the Tomb of the Unknowns.

An honor guard stands on duty at all times at the Tomb of the Unknowns. The tomb's inscription reads: "Here rests in honored glory an American soldier known but to God."
Copy.

_____

_____

_____

_____

_____

_____

_____

_____

_____

_____

_____

_____

_____

_____

Valley Forge

Valley Forge, Pennsylvania, was the campsite for General Washington and the Continental Army during the winter of 1777 and 1778.

Washington had led his army to Valley Forge after several defeats in battle. Because the Continental Congress could not give them enough supplies, the troops had little to eat or wear. Some 2,500 soldiers died in the bitter cold. Many others were too sick or weak to fight.

By spring, the loyal soldiers who had stayed with Washington were once again ready to fight for their independence against the British troops.

Copy.

_____

_____

_____

_____

_____

_____

_____

_____

_____

_____

_____

_____

_____

_____

_____

New York City

New York City is the largest city in the United States and the sixth largest in the world.

New York City is a major center for banks, industry, publishing, art and fashion. The city has so many opportunities that it is sometimes called the "Big Apple."

New York City is divided into five areas called boroughs. Each of these boroughs — Manhattan, Brooklyn, Queens, the Bronx and Staten Island — is a county of New York State.

Manhattan is the oldest borough in New York City. It is well-known for its skyscrapers, Central Park and the famous Broadway theatre area.

Copy.

The Vietnam Veterans Memorial

Name _____

The Vietnam Veterans Memorial is a national memorial to the Americans who served in the Vietnam War. The memorial is a long wall made of two sections of black marble. The names of more than 58,000 Americans killed or still missing in the Vietnam War are carved in the marble.

The memorial was designed by Maya Lin, a 21-year-old Yale University student. Over seven million dollars was raised from the American people to pay for the memorial.

The Vietnam Veterans Memorial was the idea of Jan Scruggs, a young veteran of the Vietnam War.

Today, the memorial is one of the most visited places in Washington, D.C.

Copy.

_____

_____

_____

_____

_____

_____

_____

_____

_____

_____

_____

The Oregon Trail

Name _____

The Oregon Trail brought thousands of new settlers to the far west of the United States in the mid-1800's. The trail began in Independence, Missouri, and moved westward 2,000 miles through the Great Plains and the Rocky Mountains to reach Oregon.

The Oregon Trail was first traced in 1805 by explorers and fur traders. However, it was not until 1843 that the first large group of settlers used the trail in the "Great Migration" to the Pacific Northwest.

So many people traveled the Oregon Trail to settle in Oregon that the United States was able to claim the Oregon Territory as part of our country.

Copy.

_____

_____

_____

_____

_____

_____

_____

_____

_____

_____

_____

_____

The Electoral College

The Electoral College is the group of people chosen by each state to elect the President and Vice President of the United States. The Electoral College was created in the United States Constitution. Each state determines how many representatives they may send to the Electoral College by adding their number of senators and congressional members. The state chooses these representatives in a popular election.

Although the Electoral College chooses a President, Americans still vote in a popular election. Only three times in our country's history has the most popular candidate not been elected by the Electoral College. This occured in 1824, 1876 and 1888.

Copy.

_____

_____

_____

_____

_____

_____

_____

_____

_____

_____

_____

_____

American Folklore

Many real Americans in history have become folklore heroes through the years. Legendary tales and songs have been written about them.

One of the most famous is Davy Crockett, a Tennessee frontiersman who served in the United States Congress. After his death at the Alamo in 1836, Crockett became a folk hero.

John Chapman, known as Johnny Appleseed, became well-known in the early 1800's for planting apple trees wherever he traveled. Today, Johnny Appleseed is a legendary hero.

John Henry, another folk hero, raced against a machine in digging a tunnel. A famous song tells of his victory and later his death.

Copy.

_____

_____

_____

_____

_____

_____

_____

_____

_____

_____

_____

The American Buffalo

The American buffalo, or bison, is an important part of history of America's wild west. The American buffalo once roamed in herds of thousands through America's mid-west. In 1850, over 20 million buffaloes lived on the western plains. By 1889, only 551 buffaloes lived in the United States. Many buffaloes were killed by Indians for food and clothing. Millions were killed by hunters. Finally, an effort was made to save the buffalo from extinction. Today, several thousands of buffaloes live protected on game preserves and in national parks.

The American buffalo has a large head, humped shoulders and stands close to six feet tall.

Copy.

_____

_____

_____

_____

_____

_____

_____

_____

_____

_____

_____

_____